Driftwood Forts
of the Oregon Coast

by James Herman

driftwoodforts.com
nestuccaspitpress.com
coasttime.org

Published by Nestucca Spit Press in Astoria, Oregon
An independent press publishing books about Oregon
Printed by Dave at Pioneer Printing in Newport, Oregon.
© 2014 James Herman. All images are courtesy of the
author unless otherwise listed. All rights reserved.
First Edition. ISBN 978-0-9744364-2-5

Anonymous artists make all forts unless otherwise listed.
All drawings are by the author. Layouts, design and type
treatments by the author but with generous feedback from
Danielle Fleishman. Created on location in Oregon. Made
possible by the Coast Time Artist Residency.

For Oregon

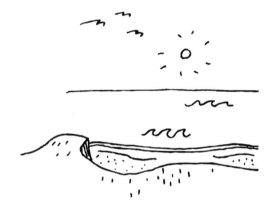

Introduction

Two-thousand nine. It was October on the Oregon Coast and the sky exuded a couple of shades of stratus gray. The husky and I were cruising down the sand at South Beach State Park when in the distance I saw a structure of some kind. I walked toward it and soon recognized the bleached façade of a somewhat circular fort with no roof. From the outside I could tell it was solidly built, logs sunk deep into the sand.

The husky and I went inside and made our inspection: a fire ring, benches, seaweed, shell, rope and feather decorations, alternating planks and a rectangular window, more like a slat, with an ocean view. The window beckoned me. I noticed a sign resting at an angle on some ancient logs. It read: "Fort Sex."

I smiled. Thank the immortal Oregon beach gods, Oswald West, Samuel Boardman, Tom McCall, Bob Bacon, Matt Kramer, Sidney Bazett and Bob Straub for creating the state's unprecedented legacy of publicly-owned beaches and protecting them from privatization— and prudery. As the famous 1967 Beach Bill decrees, "Oregon (shall) forever preserve...the free and interrupted use thereof," of the public's great birthright to recreate on the state's ocean beaches. Without these gods and without this law, no forts and no fun, unless you owned beachfront property.

Who built this wonderful structure? I wish I had. Was it indeed used for sex? Maybe I would later. Was this an art installation of some kind? I made some mental notes and took a few photographs. Later I published an account of my discovery and considered myself somewhat of an expert on the subject of driftwood forts.

Photo courtesy of Matt Love

Photo courtesy of Matt Love

Then I met James Herman and read his exquisite *Driftwood Forts of the Oregon Coast*. This is quite possibly the coolest book about the Oregon Coast I've ever encountered. In fact, I might rate James' tome as one of the coolest books in the history of Oregon literature because it is so utterly indigenous and the result of Oregon's unique heritage of conserving its ocean beaches for exclusive public use. Reading it makes me want to drop everything and go out and build a fort right now! Which is exactly what you should do.

Matt Love
Publisher, *Nestucca Spit Press*

Orientation

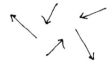

The purpose of this book is to serve on one hand as a guidebook and on the other as a travelogue regarding these ephemeral driftwood structures found along the Oregon Coast.

Wood, the primary construction material needed for these shelters is abundant in the region. It is swept up to areas of the beach just north of a tributary, and then made into driftwood over the course of several weeks or months depending on its contact with salt water, bacteria and sunlight. Once lodged on the beach, driftwood is gathered and arranged into various shelter types. FORTS.

People from all over, of all ages and education build them. Sometimes they build them for protection from the elements, but mostly just for recreation.

Driftwood amasses on shore year round but stockpiles in winter as there are fewer people using the beaches for recreation. I notice a fort-building explosion right around May and June, the months the weather improves and school gets out. It is for this reason there is quite an abundance of fort building activity in the summer.

It was right around then, but back in 2012 when I stayed in Lincoln City for the *Coast Time Artist Residency*. I was invited there so that I could enjoy some time just working on art. Many artists these days have a hard time balancing a full time job and a studio practice. I would work on sculptures and drawings in the Coast Time artist studio, using their woodshop and record collection, while intermittently taking breaks to go to the beach.

I brought with me: my large blue bag, my phone and a baseball cap (in case it got windy). On many days I combed the wrack line hoping to find useful things for the sculptures I was working on in the studio: shells, rope, beach glass, tsunami debris, wildlife and the occasional flip-flop.

One morning, there was quite a lot more beach activity than usual. Driftwood Tepee fires smoldered from the previous night's escapades, crabbers cast wide throws and there were several families holed up in tents with cocoa and boots bringing buckets back from the low tide. They were clamming.

After combing a quarter mile of beach I realized that there were driftwood forts everywhere. I went up to one. It was hulking, made of arm-width poles and giant driftwood logs for the base and it was the first of many Lean-to forts that I would find. As I left, I noticed more and more forts. I became very interested in how this activity involves a collaboration with nature and time, and the human involvement can span generations. One fort can stand while having had many different people work on it. It could have stood a whole season only to come apart and to have someone else pick up the parts to make it better, different and their own. This cycle continues for as long as there are free public beaches for humans to wander and explore and build forts for fun.

By studying the iconographies of these shelters it is evident that they differ in artistic involvement and collaboration with the landscape. Many of them only require a few limbs to complete, while others necessitate dozens. Few, if any fasteners, are used in their construction, so the fort builders must have a keen awareness of balance, surface and structural geometrics.

While on the Coast, one is constantly reminded of time's effect on their surroundings. Where ravaged beach house shingles shake and rust collects in front of your own eyes, the tides pull in and out leaving scattered remnants of their course. On shore, these structures can stand the test of days, weeks and months until they are blown down or recommissioned by the next anonymous artist. They have credence only because they are built to serve a tangible need for their designers and often are only built to last that amount of time.

They stand as relics of experiences past.

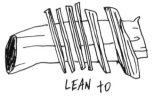

LEAN to

Tepee

A-FRAME

DUGOUT

RotuNDa

CLUSTER

BURNER

OBELISK / FLAGPOLE

CORRAL

SHaCk

Types

The following are studies of every fort type found along the Oregon Coast. Each one is distinct in the drawings, and yes, many of the photos in the book are exemplary of the truest form of said fort type. This however isn't always the case, and that is why I created fort types. Early on, when I began documenting these forts, I became intrigued by the process of categorization for each fort. This process of giving a name to something so free-form seemed like a challenge to me. Certainly some of the forts documented here are neither one type of fort, more than any other. They exist as just pure fort. Usually these are the best kind of forts. They are the kind of forts that embody many fort types and architecture, and survival shelters, classically and effortlessly. These forts exist as archetypal assemblages in the advances of fort iconography. They are master forts.

A-frame

A fort with two sloped sides that form the roof. Sometimes called a double Lean-to, this fort is very similar to many wilderness survival shelters, which makes it such a classic fort. *(See pages 60–61)*

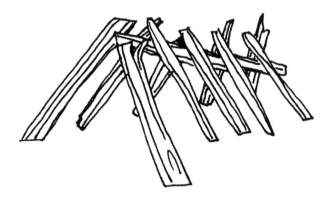

Lean-to

Again a classic fort, because its form is based on wilderness survival shelters. This fort is unique to the Coast and the Northwest in general because it requires such huge driftlogs, or root snags to lean wood against. *(See page 59)*

Dugout

Happens to be a hole dug in the ground with a wooden roof. The Dugout is a fort type for those who want to get their fingernails full of sand, or for those who want to break the *Driftwood Forts Association*'s rules by using tools, like a shovel. One must dig! *(See pages 96-97)*

Rotunda

In which the overall plan for the fort is round. It is built by standing several pieces of driftwood together, side-by-side and continuing so until they create a circle, completing the roundish shape.

Shack

Has four walls and usually a roof. The Shack can have a sloped or pitched roof. A great many treasures I have found inside of this fort type: plastic bottles, nets, beer cans, a pipe, makeup kits, leftovers, a thermos with remnants of cocoa, a kid's kite and a dollar. This makes me wonder if this is the most useful fort type? Or maybe something about it has magical functionality? How does the shack get so much use?

(See pages 122-127)

Corral

This type is more often found than made. They do get made but it seems almost like a subconscious effort. Primarily this fort designates a space for congregation. I think that it serves to stash towels and other beach items for recreation. The fort is completed in many ways by the unconscious involvement of its creators to place and pile their belongings on driftlogs and rocks.

(See pages 92-93)

Tepee

The Tepee enchants. It's a conical
frame fort, in which all beams
point upwards toward a central
axis. It exists in Westerns, and
is as embedded in the history
of our country as much
as baseball or apple pie.
(See page 29)

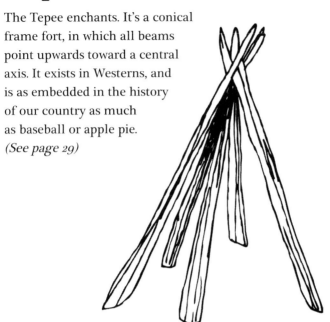

Cluster

A highly irregular but common
fort. It's a fort comprised of many
types of forts, or a fort that is hard
to classify. *(See pages 38–39)*

Burner

This is what happens when there is an already existing fort that has been burned, or when part of the driftwood used in the fort's construction has been burned, or if the fort has a fire pit (which it should… the best ones do). Essentially, a Burner is any kind of fort that has fire as a central part. It can sometimes be a Burner Shack, or a Burn-out.
(See pages 36–37)

Obelisk / Flagpole

Like the flagpole this is not necessarily a fort type, but it is a common element of fort building. They are flagpoles without flags. The Egyptian obelisk is a mysterious structure and is thought to have served as a beacon for travelers. Some have been found to catch the sun's rays at a certain point in the year and reveal secrets. In our case they may point to a fort, or even reveal a secret. *(See page 125)*

Official Rules

These rules were designated by the *Driftwood Forts Association* in 2014 to ensure that driftwood fort building will continue to be a fun and engaging activity for all ages.

I will go on to add that fort building is so much about working with what you have and that these rules really are here more as guidelines and differ very little in what anyone would actually do when building a driftwood fort.

DRIFTWOOD

FORTS ASSOCIATION

In an official fort building contest you will be judged on the following:

1 *Use only materials found on or near the beach.*

2 *No glues, screws, nails, or fasteners of any kind unless they're found on the beach.*

3 *Nothing new may be used. The tides and time must have touched your materials.*

4 *Any number of hands may work on a fort. However, when being judged in a contest this will be taken into account.*

Style: This can be interpreted as your own style, but also the fort's. How does it reflect you, your interests? Does it look good?

Materials: Does your fort use a diversity of materials? Or, is it purely driftwood? How does this relate to the styling and your own vision for the fort, and its purpose? How much wood did you use?

Types: What type of fort did you build? How well of a job did you do making it an example of that type? Or how well have you hybridized several fort types?

The furthest north one can go in Oregon is Clatsop Spit–a must for fort builders. There are three areas you can park that have beach access. I would recommend checking them all out, but area C is the best. It grants you access to the north shore of the spit, a lookout tower and plenty of driftwood.

The forts I found along the spit were super sized. Each one seemed to be made of driftwood from trees at least 100 years old, having an air of permanency.

Someday I hope to find a fort built on the end of the spit.

Astoria

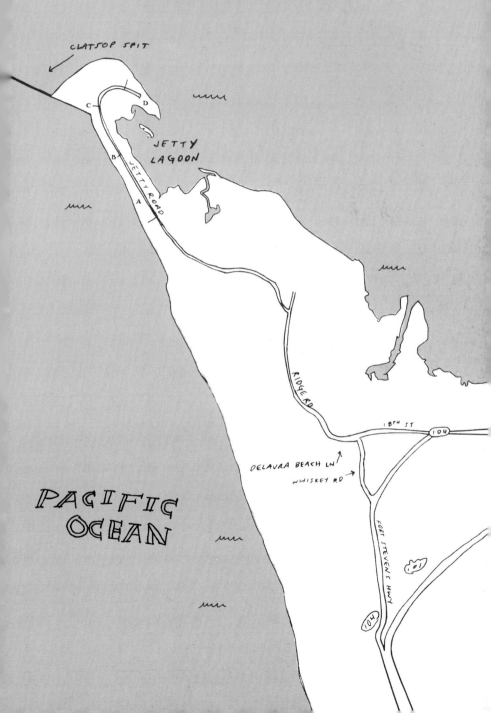

CLATSOP SPIT

C D

JETTY LAGOON

B

JETTY ROAD

A

RIDGE RD

18TH ST 104

DELAURA BEACH LN

WHISKEY RD

PACIFIC OCEAN

FORT STEVENS HWY

101

104

Driftwood. It originates from time and the tides. Trees, limbs, logs, then branches, in that order. The hierarchical arrangements of their parts gestate in the waters of the Pacific, and are reanimated by curious souls and inventive wanderers into driftwood forts.

Each time I find one it's like the first. The scenic and sandy 363 mile-long stretch of Earth known as the Oregon Coast is home to thousands of such things.

The driftwood fort is an indisputable form. Its function is open to interpretation. Likely shelter, but other more creative uses await. The wind, cold and rain all become antagonists in the story of this driftwood fort's construction.

Those limbs, logs and branches traveled that river and out into the ocean to circumnavigate the great waters of the Pacific, breaking free of the Davidson Current only to end back ashore and reformulated into an ad hoc arrangement of bodies. A whole construction, made up of parts of many others, these conglomerations bear the marks of their histories, their travel scars and battle wounds.

Some limbs in a fort's construction have been used for previous forts. Partially set aflame, or drenched in beer, each piece of the fort has its own history and essentiality to the overall design.

Pretty cool cave-like entrance made from an uprooted tree.

This page: Lean-to / Clatsop Spit, Astoria / Driftwood, cardboard and *Milwaukee's Best.*

Bottom Left: Cluster / Clatsop Spit, Astoria / Driftwood

Though this European beach grass is an invasive species, it serves to protect nearby roads, homes and towns from erosion.

Check out these huge rocks! According to the Driftwood Forts Association's official rules these are permitted on your fort so long as you found them on the beach.

This fort is an A-frame with a flanked drift-column entryway.

Some forts are built and remain
intact for months while new builders take stabs at
reconfiguring them for their own purposes, as other
forts are built just as fast as they are blown down or
burnt to coals.

Fire seems to be as much a part of the fort as water.
It must be something about the sun, the beach and
its proximity to the water. Some cosmic force? The
fort will eventually become a site for fire or itself
will be set ablaze. These Burners, or Burn-outs can
be anything from a few burnt logs to the remains
of a campfire near a fort. The burnt remains are
called drift-coal and can be used as a drawing
implement. Many fort builders will sign their forts
or give them a title. *(See "Fort Sex" in Introduction)*

I am uncertain as to which fort type this massive structure embodies but it surely deserves its place in this book. Located just behind the South Jetty and near the entry to recreation area C.

Expert driftwood stacking, weaving and layering to create a wall with interlocking corners.

Cluster and stacking configuration as a roof. Saw marks on the bottommost log.

Driftwood stacked on top of itself in the fashion of log cabin building. I wonder what those small driftwood sticks leaning up against the fort wall could be used for?

Chainsaw cut logs and driftwood stacked onto Tepee hybrid enclave. Expert fort builders freely use various elements from each fort type to create exciting hybrids.

The best way to make a wall is to place driftwood poles into the sand at common verticals, making posts. Next, run driftwood horizontally between the two posts. If one piece isn't long enough, use two butted end-to-end. Repeat.

Where does the driftwood come from? For instance, here you see a cut straight through the driftlog which indicates that it was done with a saw. Likely this was from a sawmill. Or here above it, this one is square around its edges so it was a railroad tie or some kind of building material.

Continue on stacking driftwood like this and you could eventually create a driftwood domed roof!

Gulls fly above and land on driftwood forts to check in. They have a view of driftwood forts unlike anyone else. They are the great fort mappers of the Pacific. One gull has flown from fort to fort, landing on each one as it goes, it collects a fort inventory: Shack, Cluster, Rotunda, Tepee…

These locales are popular to visit for many reasons other than driftwood fort building. But I have found they also have quite a bit of fort activity as well. It seems that when on the Coast, wherever there are people, there are forts.

In some of the following photographs, I found forts that seemed to have fallen apart or were picked apart by other hungry builders–forts that remained as a mere frame but were brought back to life and function through the simple twist of the imagination of the human. By hanging a beach towel on a drift-pole end, the frame becomes useful again.

Manzanita has an immense sea of driftwood piled up on the north shore of its beach and hardly any forts! I don't know why there are all these interconnected fort piles on the shore but very few people utilize this source of driftwood for downshore fort building.

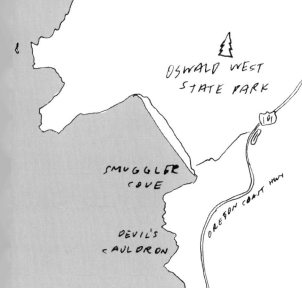

OSWALD WEST
STATE PARK

SMUGGLER
COVE

DEVIL'S
CAULDRON

OREGON COAST HWY

101

101

Oswald West
and
Manzanita

PACIFIC
OCEAN

MANZANITA

Swirling and spiraling out into
the ocean, driftwood is soaked and salted then pushed back ashore
by heavy northwesterly winds. It tumbles onto the beachhead along
with other precious fort building material: flotsam, jetsam, agates,
glass floats and shells. All this material gathers at the wrack line. This
divine culmination of offshore ocean debris is where one would find
much of the driftwood on a beach.

The wrack line also marks the beach. A wrinkly wooden–twisted wand, it holds the history of the beach. Billions of high tides and low tides where generations of families, friends and their activities swirl into composite cultural histories. The beach is a scrapbook. Driftwood is the architecture that forms the stage of those histories. From the Native Americans to the European pioneers, driftwood has been essential to the fabrication of improvised shelter and other multitudinous faculties.

This page and previous: Manzanita driftwood piles.

Left: Cluster / Oswald West State Park / Driftwood, patterned blanket, towel, rock and softsided cooler.

Bottom: Cluster / Oswald West State Park / Driftwood, towels, surfboard bag, milk crate and other assorted sundries.

Following pages: Cluster / Manzanita / Driftwood, umbrella, towel, rock, kite, cooler, shovel, shoes, chairs, *Monster* energy drink and skull.

Nice cupholder, though.

Though it may be in its early stages, this is not an official Driftwood Forts Association fort! The blatant shovel use, and look at those chairs–who needs them when there are perfectly good driftlogs! These beachcombers are not utilizing this beach to its fullest.

Do this for me if you find a derelict fort: place a piece of fallen driftwood back onto the fort. Make it yours, make it ours.

The lifespan of a fort is often in the mind of its builder. They gather logs and fashion them in a manner that suits the day's activity. Possibly, most likely in a furtive afternoon's burst of ingenuity and immediacy, the fort is formed to serve as a Capitol for the builder; a freeform fortress for beer drinking that is also a culminating stage for the campfire-lit activities at night. Christening the fort with the crack of a can of Olympia, the spark of a match, or the hanging of beach towels–the fort is yours!

Photo taken facing EAST

Lean-to / Neskowin / Driftwood SOUTH BY SOUTHWEST

A-frame / Neskowin / Driftwood, netting, lumber and Fukushima foam.

Dugout (in progress) / Neskowin / Driftwood, bodyboards and sand tools.

Cluster / Neskowin / Driftwood

At times the fort is a refuge. It is a home and keeper of things. Living and breathing. The protection it provides is aged-looking and grey. The great already worn shelter. It is a hand-me down homestead.

From left to right:
Tepee
Lean-to
Lean-to
A-frame
Dugout / Burn-out
A-frame
Cluster
Cluster
Lean-to
Cluster
Cluster

Lincoln City has Taft Park where one could build forts for a lifetime and never run out of driftwood. A truly amazing beach, and the inspiration for the book.

PACIFIC OCEAN

Lincoln City

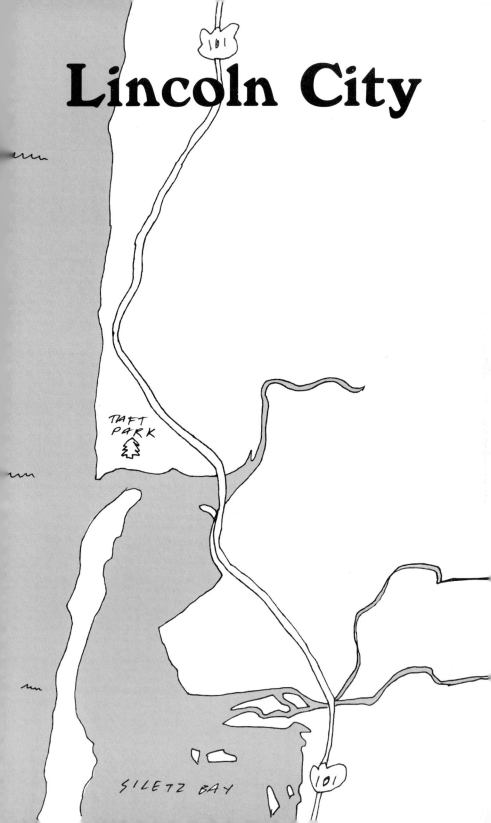

101

TAFT
PARK

SILETZ BAY

101

Facing EAST

Facing WEST

Facing NORTH BY NORTHEAST

Above: A-frame / Lincoln City / Driftwood, shipwood, lumber and pipe.
Across: Cluster, Lean-to and Corral / Taft Park / Lincoln City / Driftwood

Sometimes fort building becomes an archaeological excavation. The fort is buried. It's a skeleton, broken and folded into the dunes, drift and grey backdrop of the Pacific. What great mystery lies in the frames of this derelict fort? You can plot the trusses, yet there are missing fill boards, some of the posts may be intact. These big driftlogs, are unmovable by the tides. These posts are heavy and black, displaying burnt marks in the time-lapse of the Coast. They stand unchanging. Ancient. Many forts begin with this kind of log (the kind that doesn't ever move). They exist on a glacial time scale.

Tepee / Siletz Bay / Lincoln City / Driftwood

Tepee / Taft Park / Lincoln City / Driftwood, stump and broken pipe.
Facing SOUTHEAST

Top: NORTHWEST
Left: SOUTHEAST
Right: SOUTHWEST

How many pieces of driftwood are in this fort?

This fort's entry is sparse, leaving it susceptible to wind.

Charcoal remains are used to draw and scribe onto forts. Give the fort a name or draw a pattern.

Cluster / Siletz Bay / Lincoln City / Driftwood, bricks, plywood, pouch and pocket mirror.

Dugout / Taft Park / Lincoln City / Driftwood and lumber.

Dugout / Lincoln City / Driftwood

The ability to freely build forts on the beach is not a given right. One must come from somewhere other than the great state of Oregon to know this. Woe to those weary fort enthusiasts who are stuck in Southern California where you must pay to even see the beach, pay even more to spend an afternoon there. I'm not saying that one can't build driftwood forts there. It's just very difficult.

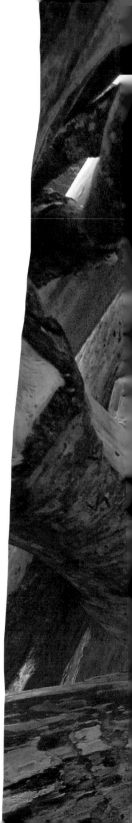

Across: **Lean-to / Cutler City / Lincoln City**

Above: **Various / Wecoma Beach / Lincoln City**

Fallen tree / Taft Park / Lincoln City

Cluster, Lean-to / Oceanlake / Lincoln City / Driftwood

Literature employs several kinds of 'conflict' to make the plot interesting for readers. There is Man versus Man conflict, Man versus Society, Man versus Nature, and Man versus Himself. These 'conflicts' are not exclusive per book either; one book may have several kinds of 'conflict' in order to tell its story. Fort building is the same way, except that, I would like to abolish 'conflict' and replace it with collaboration. I set out to write this book because I was so excited by all the different kinds of collaboration that happens in fort building, and it just so happens that these kinds of collaboration are the very kinds of conflict one can study in literature. Conflict makes for good books, not good forts.

Forts that remain on the beach and become derelict are then rebuilt or repurposed. This is a collaboration between Man and nature. Since Nature and time can move driftlogs or weather parts of a fort, they too are collaborators, but less so in this specific instance. There is also the type of collaboration in which Man is simply just working with Nature to build his shelter, his fort. This activity is increasingly at risk in our global culture, where products are mass-produced and shipped here, there, everywhere. A simple engagement with Nature in the finding and building of a fort is rewarding to many of us, as it is a very different way of selecting what you need for a project. The wood is twisted and broken in its own unique way and you, the builder will have to figure out how it contributes to the overall plan of the fort's construction. But what about the other kinds of collaboration? Man and Society? Could this be like the Southshorians in South Beach, Newport? Or is it more like a driftwood fort building festival?

Fort luck is when you find something inside of a fort. Usually it's left behind trash, sometimes it's a trinket, other times it's a treasure. I found a bottle of Evan Williams once.

There must be something magical about the waters of the Pacific at the mouth of the Siuslaw, because I have never seen better forts than at the North Jetty of the Siuslaw River.

I know it's confusing that they name the state park after the south side of the Jetty. But believe me, all the driftwood you could ever want in the world will be on the north side. Go look.

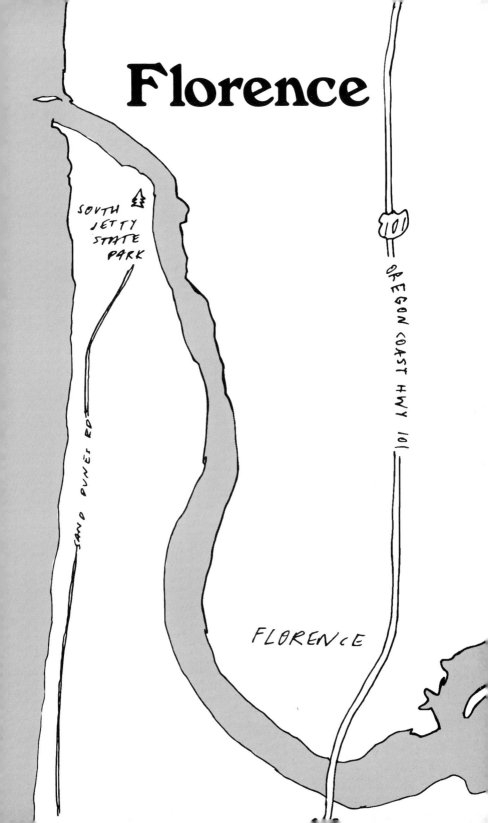

Shack (in progress) / Harbor Vista County Park,
Florence / Driftwood, ship wood, lumber and driftlog.

Tepee and A-frame / Harbor Vista County Park, Florence / Driftwood

Something deep and dark runs through the forts here. It's not a bad thing. There's just an undertow of dark creative fort energy here, which is bolstered by the stacked up and heavy driftwood on the beach. The forts are smoky and talk to you, even if you aren't listening.

I photographed these forts right after an enormous storm in late March.

Also, note the saw marks on this driftlog. It must've come from a mill and floated down the river and out into the ocean.

If this occurs on the entry of your fort it is called a sculpted portal.

Opposite: A shack and the markings on
its interior / Florence / Driftwood

These two "rooted" stumps serve as a base from which to push other logs and drift-poles up against.

Notice the flagpole? Use swim trunks or a towel as a flag. Also, notice how they built a second room for additional storage or for separate sleeping quarters? What else could it be used for?

These pieces of burnt driftwood are likely from a fort builder's fire.

Many people will find new and different uses for each fort left on the beach. One man's tuna sandwich-eatin' Shack is another's love Shack. Many forts even begin this way. The leftovers from a previous fort become the ignition for an entirely new enterprise.

This action of taking something already existing and building something new out of it is just as authentic as building from scratch. Each new imprint of a new designer/builder's touch to the life of the wood and the location of the fort on the beach is what makes a fort a fort. The fact that hundreds of beachwalkers have potentially touched, used or contributed to the building of the same fort and passed it on! Even though the State Parks Department are required to tear down forts, they don't! They build them too!

The longevity of the fort's life is twice or threefold here in Oregon, and it is only possible as long as we defend this great birthright of our people. Oregon beaches are unique, unlike anywhere else. There is riprap, but at least there are no stores, or casinos and junk, just sand, rocks and waves, and driftwood!

Newport is rumored to once have had gigantic Rotunda forts in the Yaquina Bay State Recreation area. It remains a legend.

Newport

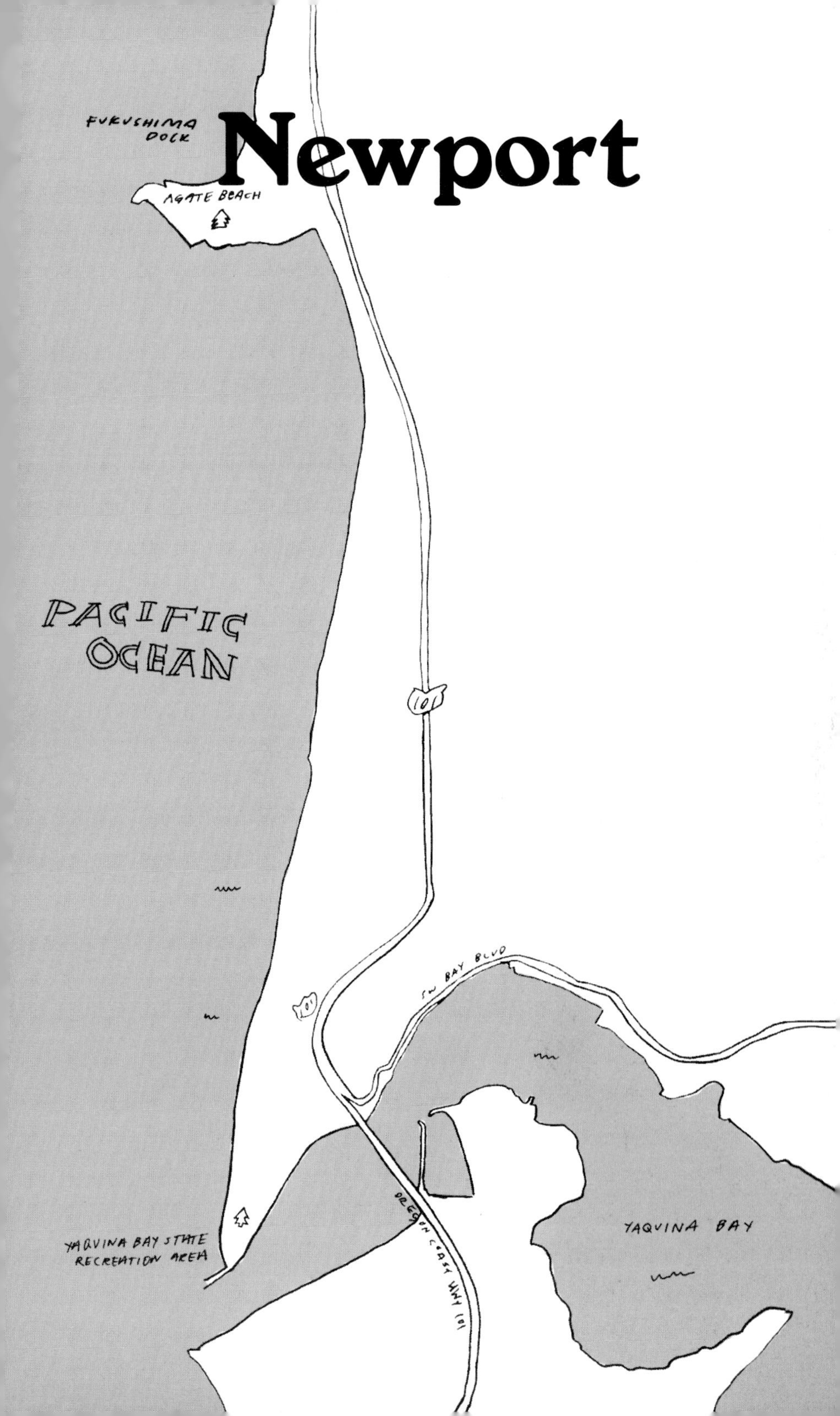

FUKUSHIMA
DOCK

AGATE BEACH

PACIFIC
OCEAN

101

101

SW BAY BLVD

YAQUINA BAY

OREGON COAST HWY 101

YAQUINA BAY STATE
RECREATION AREA

Facing SOUTH BY SOUTHEAST

Above and Right: Cluster, Corral / Yaquina Bay State Recreation Area /
Newport (1.5 miles north of South Beach) / Driftwood, plywood and stump.

Facing NORTHWEST

Someway, somehow, someday, there will be a musical fort, brandished with rusting cans, beach glass, rope and its own exotic orchestration of instruments. There will be kelp guitar and bass. Heavy and deep thumping and twanging. The glass bottles and floats are whistles and chimes. They improvise with the wind and rip mean solos. The frame of this fort is a hardened and dense driftwood marimba. It keeps time.

The soul of this music runs deep into the Pacific with veins of the Siuslaw and Siletz. It jams out with the tides and harmonizes with the seasons. This music is unlike anything you've ever heard.

Dugout / Yaquina Bay State Recreation Area / Driftwood

Dugout / Yaquina Bay State Recreation Area / Driftwood, lumber, flotsam and *Dasani* bottle.

Tepee / Yaquina Bay State Recreation Area / Driftwood

South Beach State Park is just south of the Yaquina Bay Bridge (HWY 101) and is host to a semi-permanent fort building community. I found several forts at South Beach and no shortage of driftwood.

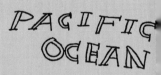

South Beach

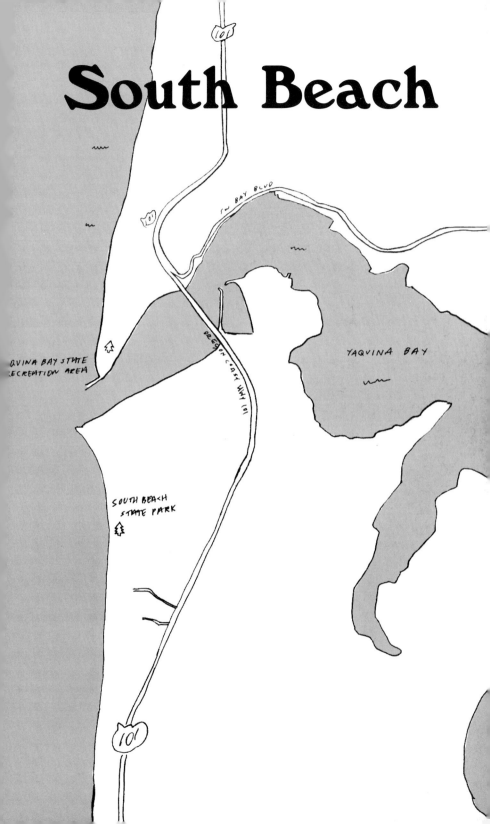

101

SW BAY BLVD

101

YAQVINA BAY

OREGON COAST HWY 101

QVINA BAY STATE
RECREATION AREA

SOUTH BEACH
STATE PARK

101

Dugout / South Beach / Driftwood

Cluster / South Beach / Driftwood

A-Frame / South Beach / Driftwood

Cluster / South Beach / Driftwood

On a foggy overcast day, that's when the Oregon Coast is in its purest form. Scan the horizon, all you will find is forts.

Detail of the bench

Picnic tables and wind barrier fort. The added flair of the checkered tablecloth may take away from the fort's natural charm but it serves a sanitary function and shouldn't be up for as critical a review as the rest of the fort.

Each year these "Southshorians" (as they refer to themselves in the laminated note on the fort's entry) build a giant wind barrier fort, equipped with fish-prepping tables, benches, a fire pit and more (*See previous pages*). This massive structure varies from year to year, but is firmly seated above the wrack line, where the tides have a more difficult time destroying it. It remains mostly intact, throughout the year, with modifications as they see fit.

My fort scout dog immediately saw the gigantic fort as we broke over the dunes and headed down onto the sand. A unique-looking structure emerged as I approached. I felt compelled to further examine it. What I found was a smaller wind-breaking dugout about 300 feet in front of the Southshorian fortress. I thought: what a brilliant new concept! This truly was remarkable, as I had found hundreds of forts in my time but never two that seemed to be part of the same one. A compound. It was almost as if this small fort was an outpost of sorts for other activities that may go on in the fortress. The interconnectedness of these two structures speaks volumes to how we as people can use our surroundings and those around us.

I couldn't classify the fort as anything but a
Raft. The broad platform, lodged in proximity to another fort could
only be such a thing. I imagine this raft frame is either a work in
progress or possibly has already made one sailing attempt, and is back
to shore for repairs. If I were constructing the Raft, I would be sure to
carry extra water with me and attach inner tubes for added buoyancy.

Left: Raft / South Beach / Driftwood

Right: Corral, campfire / South Beach / Driftwood, stump, plastic buckets and enameled coffee cup.

Building

I set out to build what I later began calling the
ten year (tenure) fort on a gray morning in South
Beach, Oregon. I had traveled from Eugene with a
good friend, one from way back, who was ready for
some fort building on the Oregon Coast. We met
Matt at his house, gathered ourselves and a few
beers, and headed down the beach.

We walked along, the grey backdrop hanging a
hundred yards in front of us as we set our course,
reveling in the cool summer breeze. Matt had
scouted some driftwood piles that he thought I
would be interested in for the fort. One or two
miles out, we found a fort, and then another. This
was a good sign. They were small, one wind barrier
fort, and one that looked like the remains of a great
fort. I knew we were getting close. Someone had
left a three wood golf club and a handful of golf
balls for a mediative ocean bound-ball whacking
session. I imagined we'd run into him or her later.

Another mile out I could see a creek and then piles
of driftwood, driftlogs, lumber, everything. I mean
this was epic. We walked into the creek and began
examining the location, the quantity of wood, and I
knew this was it. Matt was right. This was the spot.
We had a literal ton of wood.

So where does one begin?

This page and previous: Driftpile of which we used to
construct our fort.

Top: Corral and wind barrier / South Beach /
Driftwood and rocks.

Bottom: Cluster / South Beach / Driftwood

This post was made by digging into the sand and placing a driftlog in it. We later reinforced the base with piles of rocks.

We began with a small A-frame entryway. As we built it out towards the main part of the fort we placed more driftwood along the base of it to reinforce the frame of the fort.

There's no right way to build a fort. Or at least I don't know of one. We just started picking up driftlogs and poles and seeing what we had. All of the process was very intuitive. I found myself looking at a piece of driftwood then imagining where it would best serve the fort. Conversation about the fort was like, "Hey, what if we made this area an entry? If we used these bigger fatter ones to form a peak and continue stacking them along to make it a tunnel?"

"I'm down."

And more gathering and stacking and placing. I was pleased with how we chose to orient our entry facing south to avoid those heavy beach winds from the north. The term 'orientation' or 'to orient' came from architecture, as many ancient temples had entries facing the east which (back then) in Rome or Egypt faced Asia, the real orient. Fort building does reference architecture but is much more temporal and should be thought of as ritual, or something practiced, that is not institutionalized.

We had finished our entry and began to think about how to continue.

Fort building reminded me of a lecture the architect Fujimoto gave called "Cave or Nest." The nest is built and well suited for people, whereas the cave is found and people make due. The nest has a specific function and is fully realized by its makers. Whereas the cave is already built, it is a found kind of architecture and its functions and uses are discovered once occupied, it is more creative. Western architecture, our own houses, apartments and office buildings are nests. We choose bedroom, living room, kitchen and so on to accommodate our needs. The cave allows for a more communal and creative discourse on designating areas and their functions.

Is a fort a cave or a nest? Maybe it's a found nest or a built cave?

I imagine seeing our fort from the sea, on a sailing vessel as a different race or species, as if I were encountering driftwood forts for the first time, as an outsider, an explorer, a conquistador. I tried to un-see it and see it again. I thought about the pioneers, the Native Americans, the Spanish, and what did they think when they saw their first driftwood fort? Back in the fort on South Beach, we begin building the main chamber of the fort. Ideas about its function are discussed.

"We need a writing studio and a sauna."

"How about a library?"

The ways things were progressing we have could kept building and building to accommodate every activity under the sun. We settled on a modest library and thought that we should leave the rest open to interpretation. The way we were simultaneously building and brainstorming possibilities for the fort seemed only natural.

We were balancing logs but also balancing the possibility of what we wanted to build. The ways driftwood fits together allows for a some control and customization of what one is building, but the scale at which of fort building happens has its restrictions. Several factors determine this, mostly the fact that you aren't working with tools or fasteners, but also that the wood is found, and usually twisted and broken.

A fort build is slow to start, then accumulates speed and mass, only to taper off and slow down towards the end. Many pieces of driftwood were carried and placed at this point, and the sun had arched its way over us, now casting rays across the ocean and onto the fort.

The roof resembled a wavy gravy geodesic dome with cross supports laid one across from another, forming and formulating into triangular truss braces. Driftwood running 12 to 40 inches long and of little width was implemented as a lightweight and effective rooftop. These drift-sticks would fill and span the triangular truss braces creating our mosaic patch work roof sheeting, of alternating variegation.

The fort was complete. All that was left was for us to christen it...

The next day I woke up warm next to where our driftwood fire had burned. The sun felt close to my face and the ocean was calm. I gathered my things and wandered back into town. On my walk I wondered if this fort really could last ten years. Attain literal tenure and become an institution. I could see it becoming a protected site, like a historic lighthouse or a wild bird refuge. I have ambitions for the fort. It could happen. The fort is located about three miles down from South Beach State Park. It is high up on the shore, back against the European beach grass and near that creek where all the driftwood collects year round. I want it to become an ever-expanding fort, something that generations of people visit and add to. Maybe eventually I would take up residence and the title of caretaker. Until then, it would be carried by the hands of hundreds of beachcombers, each contributing a modest limpet to the branch we placed near the entry, ornamenting and even adding to the structure with more driftwood.

Together we could build it to span the length of an entire housing development. A mile in either direction, with a bald eagle nest in the middle at the highest lookout point. The ten-year fort offers visitors the possibility of adding to its massive structure and its legacy: an ongoing public art work, the largest ever made of driftwood and no fasteners.

And it didn't cost a thing.

Our fort's burnt driftwood totem collection and A-frame entry.

How-to

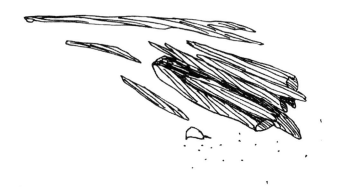

This guide gives you in-depth instructions on how to build the A-frame driftwood fort, how to turn it into a Tepee, and then how to turn that into a Rotunda. It also provides some simple steps for building all the other fort types!

Scan the Coast, and use the wrack line to lead you to more driftwood. A good amount of driftwood is required to make a sturdy fort, one that will keep the wind at bay. These giant driftlogs can sometimes make a quick Lean-to if they are fat enough. The Lean-to looks like the classic "fallen tree" shelter famously revealed in D.C Beard's SHELTERS, SHACKS, AND SHANTIES. But since you are on the Coast and can't cut down part of a tree to make a sloped roof you'll have to find something thick and tall enough to prop driftwood up against. Once you've found such a thing, create the sloped roof shape by placing driftwood, running it perpendicular from the top down into the sand, and repeating this until adequate roofing is achieved. This is a quick and easy fort but only if you have a large enough base to prop more wood up against. A fallen log, or a "snag" works; most of the Lean-tos in the book are of huge root snags and stumps. Keep in mind this fort type and many others can be "wilderness survival shelters" when insulated with moss, leaves and other foliage.

... It all began with a **Lean-to**

(1)

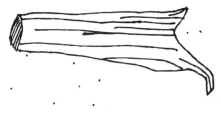

Start with a huge driftlog, or a root wad. You need something that is tall. It will make for a roomier fort.

(2)

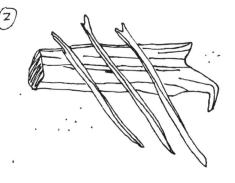

Collect driftwood and start making a roof by laying pole perpendicular to the base.

Once you have adequately filled in your roof, you are done. Use this quick simple fort for rain shelter or as protection from the blasting sand on a windy day. Note: it is possible to make this fort by using a long drift-pole to span two areas like some rocks, or a rock and a stump. Once you've spanned the distance you can lay the rest of your drift-poles perpendicularly to form the roof.

(3)

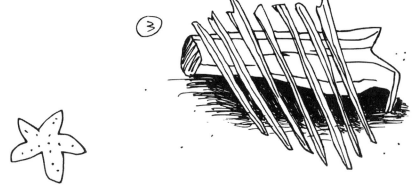

A-frame

① Begin with two drift-poles that have notches in them near the end.

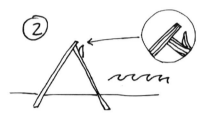

② Place two equal-length pieces of driftwood into the sand to form an "A." Be sure one of those has a notched end at the top so that you are able to do the next step.

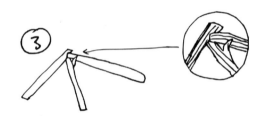

③ Now that you have an "A," using your longest piece of driftwood, lay it into the top cradle you formed when making your "A" and use the notch to help balance it. You can even push the end of it into the sand for stability.

④ Fill in the sides of the fort using more driftwood. Once you have covered both sides, your fort is complete. Give it a name, something classy like "Sea Shack" Take a picture of it and send it to me! You may win a prize.

Here's all the addresses:
info@driftwoodforts.com
facebook.com/driftwoodforts
instagram.com/driftwoodforts

An A-frame, sometimes called a double Lean-to, can be constructed by adding another side to the sloped roof of your already built Lean-to. Doubling your fort's capacity is a must for adventures with more people or animals. The other side of the fort can be used as storage, too (*See pages 124-127*). Gear, food and other sundry items can be kept dry, free and clear on this side. It is necessary to see potential and possibilities when fort building.

In order to do this, you're going to need more driftwood. Save the driftwood from your Lean-to. Gather a large pile if you can. You'll need some drift-poles that are taller than you, also. Get one that has a notch on the end, so you can lock three poles together. Next, place two pieces of driftwood that are equal size into the sand to form an "A." This will be the entrance to your fort. It helps to have someone else hold this up for you while you complete this next step.

Now that you have your "A," take the longest piece of driftwood you have and lay it into the top cradle you formed when making your "A." Push the end of it into the sand for additional stability. This should give you the classic A-frame frame.

Next, fill in the sides of your fort with all the remaining driftwood that you have collected. Done.

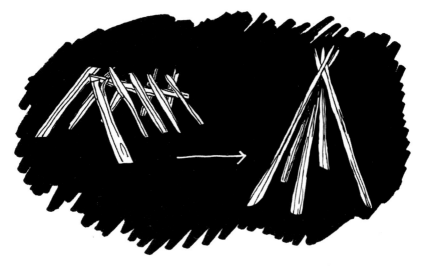

See how the A-frame can become a Tepee next!

The poles used on your sloping roof are likely of similar width and length, which makes for good Tepee poles. I suggest pulling some poles off of one side of your A-frame or finding some more and taking them down the beach, closer to the water. The sand is softer there, and it will be easier to trench down to make a solid Tepee.

This new fort type, the Tepee is constructed by arranging several drift-poles from the ground up towards a central axis point. Try balancing three poles into a tripod shape. Assembling this tripod is basic idea of the fort. Once achieved, you can then begin to fit other poles around the radius. If you are a solo fort builder, or having trouble balancing, it may help to find some kelp strands, even some rope, nothing too thick, but also of good length. Lash three poles together at the top while they lay on the ground and when you erect them, and spread them into the radius of the base of the Tepee they will hold together better. You can use this primitive lashing technique on any cluster fort types as well. It is important to practice other fastening techniques, even though the purest forts are made solely with driftwood.

It is quite remarkable when a Tepee is covered in the round with poles. Acting as a skein, it will strengthen your fort, and provide shelter from the sun, wind and rain. Crafting an entrance should be also taken into consideration when making this fort. This could be a strategic consideration and may involve many factors. For instance, you may wish to watch the sun drop into the Pacific Ocean that evening, and a view from the Tepee may be achieved by having the entrance face the ocean.

Begin with three long poles. Balance them into a tripod. Follow step two if you are having trouble.

Tepee

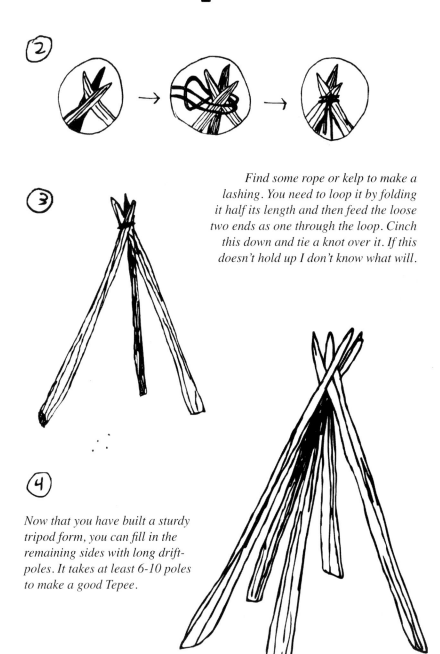

②

Find some rope or kelp to make a lashing. You need to loop it by folding it half its length and then feed the loose two ends as one through the loop. Cinch this down and tie a knot over it. If this doesn't hold up I don't know what will.

③

④

Now that you have built a sturdy tripod form, you can fill in the remaining sides with long drift-poles. It takes at least 6-10 poles to make a good Tepee.

An understanding in these first three types of forts will grant you the foundation to limitless possibilities of fort building. It seems beneficial that I describe to you what other fort types could transpire out of the understanding of these first three. The Rotunda is a more substantial fort type that could even be made into a permanent structure. The skeletons of legendary Rotunda forts on the Yaquina Bay, are buried waiting to be uncovered and built again.

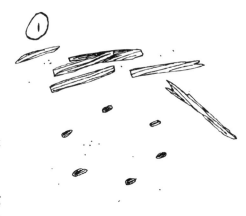

The Rotunda harkens back to early forts made by Europeans and Natives along the Northwest Coast. They have permanence and solidity to their construction and look like something out of a Western. Fences and many other modern building techniques are based off this fort type.

Begin with 6-10 drift-poles that are as tall as you want the fort to be. Dig holes in a circle or semicircle to plot out where you eventually will be sinking these poles in.

While the Rotunda has a circular floor plan with a flat roof, the Shack has a square or rectangular floor plan with a sloped roof. The Cabin is like a Shack only it has an A-frame sloped roof, a peak. Each of these are advanced fort types and require much more driftwood than an A-frame or Tepee, but happen to be just as satisfying when completed.

Rotunda

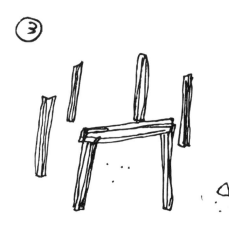

Use the holes in the sand to sink your drift-poles into. Use the collective weight and form of each pole to contribute to the overall balance and stability of the fort. Save one to span two that are at a good width to form an entry.

Fill in all sides of the Rotunda. Use everything you got. This is your chance to go big.

Once you've got all the side filled in and your entry made you are done. But if you want to get fancy you could lay long poles across the top to form a roof, making it into a more of a Shack.

Shack

This is the classic fort. Shacks are those kinds of forts that don't ever go away; they may fall apart, but someone will put them back together. Probably because of the sheer amount of driftwood involved in their construction, they stand. But if the fort's strength wanes and some wood falls off, don't fret. The wood never really leaves (unless it's burnt down). Season in and season out, wood falls off a fort, piles at its base, only to be picked up and returned to the fort by another curious fort lover. This process of returning the wood and building upon what already exists is fundamental to the collaborative aspect of the fort building phenomenon. By returning the wood you are signing your name to long list of contributors, artists and builders in the history of the fort.

①

Begin by digging four holes about the length of your arm to your elbow, or a little less. Put driftwood into these holes and fill it back up with sand, pack down. These post as we call them, will now be referred to as A, B, C, D.

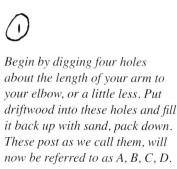

②

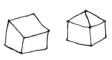

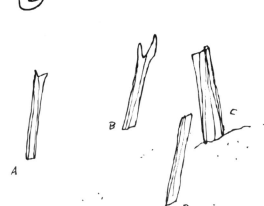

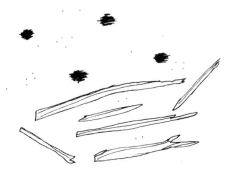

The Shack has two different roof types (see above), but for each, you must run drift-poles from the top of A to B, and from B to C, and C to D, and D to A (see 3). This is the frame of your roof! Choose which roof, either sloped or pitched.

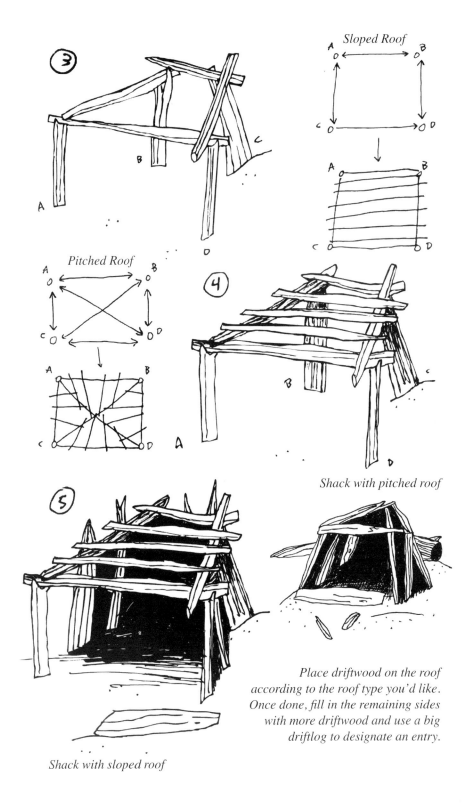

③

Sloped Roof

Pitched Roof

④

Shack with pitched roof

⑤

Place driftwood on the roof according to the roof type you'd like. Once done, fill in the remaining sides with more driftwood and use a big driftlog to designate an entry.

Shack with sloped roof

Dugout

You are going to need to dig a big hole. Tools help for this one even though they are against the rules.

Once you've got it dug out begin placing driftwood across the top, forming a roof.

One trick I have seen is that fort builders will use a driftlog or two running parallel to the hole. They put them down before placing the perpendicular running drift-poles to give the roof added height and a slant.

Obelisk / Flagpole

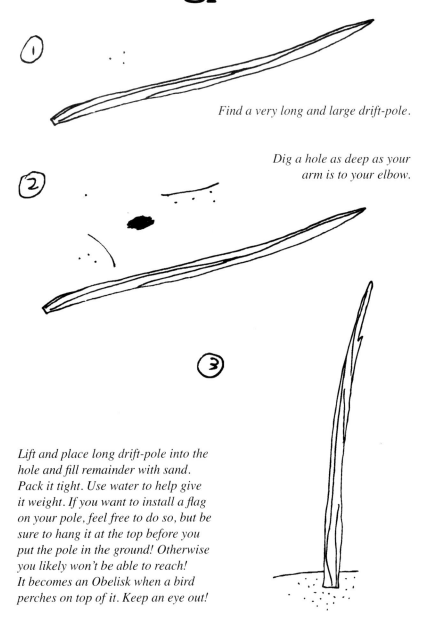

① Find a very long and large drift-pole.

Dig a hole as deep as your arm is to your elbow.

②

③

Lift and place long drift-pole into the hole and fill remainder with sand. Pack it tight. Use water to help give it weight. If you want to install a flag on your pole, feel free to do so, but be sure to hang it at the top before you put the pole in the ground! Otherwise you likely won't be able to reach! It becomes an Obelisk when a bird perches on top of it. Keep an eye out!

Corral

An intuitive person might not think about what they are going to build before they build it. Maybe they will build something based on a feeling or a hunch? There are as many of those kinds of builders as there are the opposite; these are the kind of fort builders that think out and sketch out what they are going to build before they build it.

The Corral can really start anywhere. I mean, look at the one on page 92 in Newport. This was clearly made with what materials were closest and served the immediate purpose of its builder's needs.

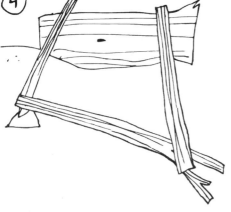

Find a driftlog, find a big rock, find a few drift-poles, and get them together. Start arranging them in a manner that quarters off a space. Trapezoidal etc...

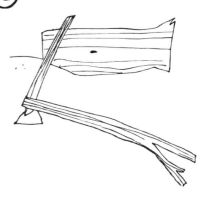

Use what's already around you. Do this as quickly as possible. Try to make your fort accommodate a party of five, loaded with beach recreation sundries.

160

Burner

Let's say for the sake of the story that I am a fort builder who thinks things through. In recent memory I was in Lorane tying a load of tree branches down to a fourteen-foot-long trailer with an old timer. I was looking at the rope, and visualizing my knot, turning the rope in my hands. The old timer chuckled, "You tie that knot like you went to college!" He took the rope out of my hand and showed me "the only knot I'll ever need." I laughed and watched him tie one heck of a trucker's knot. I went home and practiced that knot so I wouldn't forget.

Fort building can be both a thought-out activity and one that is spontaneous or based on past experiences and feeling. I like the forts where it seems like the maker placed each piece of driftwood intentionally, and at each step they thought about all the possible placements and chose the least intuitive or structural option. This dumbfounded strategy results in a very unusual fort, one that defies formal logic and possibly even gravity.

I wonder what would happen if you compared a fort like that, against one built by someone else who had meticulously planned each piece's placement? Would they look similar? Even better would be to then have them try to build each other's fort's with the same wood.

1. Build a fort, any type of fort. Or find one.

2. Next, you're going to set that fort on fire.

3. Enjoy the process, the fire, the letting go of your creation, and the warmth. Find creative uses for the charcoal remains! Write or draw with them, get some paper and make rubbings.

Quite a number of activities can be performed in a fort and with it. Use it as a camp, or a bed, or for storytelling, for loving, cooking, beer-drinking, friend-making, sharing, smoking, campfires, towel-hanging, snorkel gear-hanging, writing studio, dog leash anchor, private sanctuary and a wind shelter. It's conducive to social activities when built around a central point, like a fire-pit, for conversation, or a conversation piece, carving wood, stone sharpening, arrowhead making, hair braiding, beading, embroidering, drawing, painting, painting on driftwood, keeping warm, keeping cool, carving your initials, making kelp wands, making seaweed salads, organizing your shells, making a shell mosaic in the sand, stacking stones, tanning, fanning, jamming, bring guitars and friends, blankets and sing some songs, all of this is fun.

But none of it is as fun as building another driftwood fort!

The End

Epilogue

To Build a Fort

We carried, coaxed, hoisted, angled, positioned, buttressed, wedged and interlocked driftwood for hours and hours, into the night, fueled by beer and wine and other legal medicines and a shrimp stir fry cooked on a bonfire. We were *Lord of the Flies* and *Gilligan's Island* and the Tower of Babel and *Fear and Loathing in South Beach* all rolled into one roiling architectural circus. There were dogs, coast veterans, an aspiring social studies teacher, freaks, fire, fairies, candles, ghosts of Oswald West and Tom McCall, a typewriter, poetry, a siren, a mermaid, a mortgage broker, and the old sound of the ocean driving us mad with absurd ambition and preposterous vainglory.

Higher and higher we went one crazy July afternoon and evening and morning. We were young, ancient and unstoppable and had no blueprint guiding us to build the greatest driftwood fort in the history of the Oregon, a Colosseum, an Acropolis, a World Trade Center, an Astrodome. We hardly needed a blueprint; something deep, crustacean, and salty within our collective archetypes would draw up plans for us on the spot. "I am the sea! I am the sea!" Shouted D.H. Lawrence. We heard his ripples through the eons of aquatic Einstein time and surfed them forever in our minds.

The build culminated the mythical Season of the Driftwood Forts. I saw them everywhere this summer. I built or remodeled or decorated them everywhere. I was dreaming forts, documenting forts, extolling forts, napping, writing and wrestling hippie angels inside of forts. I wanted to live in one or become one.

We were fortified on the wonderful senseless purpose of building a master fortification, an ultimate fort, the Stepmother of All Oregon Coast Driftwood Forts, a mansion in the sand, a shelter in the rain,

crafted by hands and tides, sweat and storms, constructed from logs and planks, flotsam and jetsam, all manner of organic and man-made detritus washed ashore from denuded watersheds and an obliterated Japan. There was enough driftwood scattered around our random site to build a celebrity complex of forts, but we would erect just one, a grand wooden palace that would stand for less than an eternity and enchant anyone who happened across its crooked magnificence. We wanted every visitor to stand there, agape, then kneel, dumfounded, dizzied, blinded by the fort, and ask a million unanswerable questions of this oracle. Visitors, especially the children, would remember us forever without ever knowing who we were because our fort inspired fortitude for life and love and building the fort within not yet built.

Our leaderless leader was a man named James Herman, an artist, a writer, a photographer, a camper, a seeker, a savant, with the blood of Steve Prefontaine and Ken Kesey and Bigfoot streaming through his veins, who, would soon release the greatest book in the history of world literature on the subject of driftwood forts. I thought I was the expert and I relish being wrong in my colossal arrogance. After meeting James and hearing his vision, I became his acolyte, and well, his publisher, too. And that's what we were really doing, finishing his book, because he didn't have an ending.

At some point, we finished the fort, christened it, gave it no name to keep it all opaque and ephemeral, stepped back and marveled. The moon and stars emerged. A couple of drunks wandered through, joined us, ate red meat, switched on XM radio from a boombox and called up some classic rock, the Doors or Loverboy I think. There were hosannas all around, clouds of ceremonial smoke, streaks of blackberries and screw top sacrifices to the patron saints of weird secular monuments. Our fort—if fort is the word—was epic and magisterial to behold. It had three rooms, a roof, a studio, and a library stocked with all the good dead Romantic poets who drank port from human skulls! A rock band could have gigged inside! I was ready to book Neil Young and Crazy Horse! Neil would have played for free if only for want of trying to crumble the fort with one of his endless broadsides of feedback, kind of like a Jericho in reverse.

James got his ending.

A few days later, State Parks employees tore it down. So be it. Bureaucracies are bureaucracies. In our minds, we'll keep building that fort bigger, stronger and more ineffable, building it a thousands times over. Good play—on the beach and in life—leads to bold imagination and a bureaucracy-free soul. Besides, we still made Oregon history that day and night and confirmed the first and last axiom of driftwood fort building: nothing is permanent. That is and is not a metaphor.

Matt Love
Publisher, *Nestucca Spit Press*

Glossary

A-frame
Like a Lean-to only it has two slopes.

Beach Bill
Was passed in 1967 and made the dry sand areas of Oregon's beaches public recreation areas...forever. (*See also: Oswald West, Tom McCall*)

Bob Straub
Was an environmentalist and Oregon Governor from 1975-1979. He helped save Nestucca Spit and Cape Kiwanda from a ill-conceived plan to relocate Highway 101 down the beach.

Cabin
A fort type that resembles a wilderness cabin. It should have four walls and a roof.

Cardboard
Material made from wood pulp, processed into brown sheets used for packaging and shipping stuff

Corral
A configuration of driftwood that resembles an enclosure or fenced area. A delineation of space via log.

Devil's Cauldron
North of Manzanita in Oswald West State Park. There's an overlook of Highway 101. This would be an epic location for a driftwood fort.

Driftlog
Driftwood that is generally hulking in size, a log. (*See also: driftwood*)

Drift-lumber
Driftwood that was once lumber, like a 2 x 4. (*See also: driftwood*)

Drift-pole

Driftwood that is usually from a tree branch. *(See also: driftwood)*

Driftwood

Is wood washed a shore by the tides. It has had contact with the sea's salty water and washed its color and seasoned its appearance. You can find it on any beach, but the best parts are where a river or creek meets the ocean on the north side of the beach. In the Pacific Northwest the Davidson Current is what pushes material up the beach in that motion.

Driftwood Forts Association

Established in 2014 by James Herman for the education and promotion of driftwood fort building.

Dugout

A hole dug in the ground, sometimes with a wooden roof.

Dunes

Big hills of sand, formed by wind. Sometimes they are grassy and near the ocean.

European beach grass

Ammophila arenaria or European beach grass, was brought to Oregon in the mid 19th century to help stabilize the dunes and to protect nearby towns from storms. It has since spread all the way up to Canada, and all the way down to California. It has destroyed much of the native dune habitat in Oregon. *(Source: Wikipedia)*

Fort

A made-up place for recreation.

Fort Scout Dog

Man's best friend, also is good a finding forts. Let this guy off the leash see what he can do! My Fort Scout Dog is in the book five times, can you find every photo of him?

Lean-to

A roof with one slope.

Matt Kramer

The Oregon journalist who used his writing in 1967 to shift public opinion towards the preservation of Oregon beaches. His memorial is located in Oswald West State Park. Visit.

Matt Love

Is an author whose work has become essential to Oregon's history. He has published numerous books on the more alternative side of Oregon's history. He runs Nestucca Spit Press, an independent press publishing books about Oregon. He is also a beach freak and fort connoisseur.

Obelisk

A driftwood pole struck straight up into the sand. Serves multiple purposes i.e. flagpole...Also, references the Egyptian obelisk. (*See also: Egyptology, or the White House*)

Oregon Coast Highway 101

The major north-south highway along the Oregon Coast.

Oswald West

The Oregon governor who initiated the preservation of Oregon's beaches and birthright to its citizens. He served from 1911-1915 and conceived the beach highway law which meant that the entire wet sand area of the ocean beaches a public highway. In doing so, he prevented anyone from developing it, thus preserving it for future fort building generations.

Raft

Lashed-together driftlogs to form a vessel fit for sea or river travel. This is a very rare fort type! See South Beach section for a more detailed account of when I found one.

Rotunda

A fort with a round base plan, where the driftwood sticks straight up and down, and does not point towards the center like a Tepee.

Samuel Boardman

Was the first Oregon Parks superintendent and the father of the Oregon parks system.

Shack

Generally it's an A-frame but with side walls.

Shipwood

Driftwood that is from a wrecked ship. You can tell it is from a ship if it has a painted surface or some sort of epoxy on it. See also, driftwood.

Sidney Bazett

Yet another invaluable advocate for the preservation of Oregon's beaches. Sydney served in the legislature from 1961-1973. He was a Republican.

Siletz Bay

Located in Lincoln City. Home to the skeleton trees, host to beautiful wildlife and not to mention driftwood.

Siuslaw River

One of the longest rivers in Oregon, it ends near Florence. The river valley happens to define the timber industry in Oregon, which is why there is fantastic fort building on the north Siuslaw River jetty in Florence.

Smugglers Cove

Located in Oswald West State Park, it is a mysterious area only accessible to hikers. I think they have some forts down there!

Southshorians

A very advanced fort building community in South Beach just 1.5 miles south of Newport.

Tepee

Conical frame structure usually covered with a tarp or canvas material. Covering material not necessary when building a fort. Use driftwood.

The Rock

The Rock is located on a pullout on the west side of highway 101 on your way to Manzanita from Oswald West State Park. It is a large rock with a plaque that commemorates Governor Oswald West's brilliant idea to make Oregon's beaches a 'highway' which in turn set into motion their preservation for future generations, until Governor Tom McCall could seal the deal in 1967 with his Beach Bill.

The Rock reads:

YE SIGHT OF SAND AND SKY AND SEA
HAS GIVEN RESPITE FROM YOUR DAILY CARES
THEN PAUSE TO THANK

FORMER GOVERNOR OF OREGON OSWALD WEST (1911-1915)

BY HIS FORESIGHT
NEARLY 400 MILES OF THE OCEAN SHORE
WAS SET ASIDE FOR PUBLIC USE
FROM THE COLUMBIA RIVER ON THE NORTH
TO THE CALIFORNIA BORDER ON THE SOUTH.

THIS MARKER IS ERECTED AND DEDICATED
BY THE CITIZENS OF OREGON
TO COMMEMORATE
THIS OUTSTANDING ACHIEVEMENT
IN THE CONVERSATION OF NATURAL RESOURCES.

Tom McCall

The famous Oregon Governor who in 1967 signed the Beach Bill ensuring free and uninterrupted public access to the entirety of Oregon beaches.

Wrack line

Wrack line or tidal wrack provides an ever changing path to follow along the Coast. Since it is created by the debris that is washed up shore during high tide it varies daily.

← WAVES

← SHORE

← DRIFT

← WRACK

Beachcombers will walk up and down this wrack line to find precious shells, moon snails, slippers, sponges, feathers, even agates. But most of all it's a great place to start building a fort.

Yaquina Bay

The famous bay which Newport is settled around. The state recreation area is fine for fort hunting and building, but I would recommend driving south on Highway 101 till you get to South Beach. That's where the real fort building action is.

Join the driftwood fort revolution by sending me any and all driftwood fort pictures that you have taken on the Coast!

I will award those with the best fort photo each month by featuring it on the driftwoodforts.com website's homepage and by sending them a prize which could be a book, or button set, or who knows!

Send your fort photos directly to me!
info@driftwoodforts.com
or find me on facebook.com/driftwoodforts
or even better @driftwoodforts on instagram!

Forts for life.

I've drawn considerable influence from several authors whose works stand as classics of their genre.

SHELTERS, SHACKS, AND SHANTIES
by D.C. Beard

THE IMMENSE JOURNEY
by Loren Eisley

BUSHCRAFT
by Richard Graves

SHELTER
by Lloyd Kahn

SOMETIMES A GREAT NOTION
by Ken Kesey

WOODCRAFT AND CAMPING
by George W. Sears Nessamuk

WILD TREES
by Richard Preston

I'D RATHER BE BEACHCOMBING
by Bert Webber

THE FOXFIRE JOURNALS
by Eliot Wigginton

BEACHCOMBING THE PACIFIC
by Amos L. Wood

...Further Forts

Though Oregon is the world capital for fort building, there are other fort-centric locales in this big world. The following is a list to get you started, and you can also check in with me for more at driftwoodforts.com

LADONIA
North-west Skåne, Sweden. In the 1980s artist Lars Vilks constructed two driftwood fortresses, Nimis and Arx, which weigh nearly 100 tons and are the subject of many legal disputes.

HANDS ON CHILDREN'S MUSEUM
Olympia, WA. Year round outdoor driftwood fort construction area!
hocm.org

NORTHERN CALIFORNIA
Jenner Beach, Navarro River Beach and Big River Beach.

WASHINGTON
Olympia National Forest, La Push, Lummi Island and Orcas Island.

Acknowledgements

To start, I really must say how formational the Coast Time Artist Residency was for me. Donald Morgan, took it upon himself to get me into the residency as a guinea pig, which is where I began the earliest version of this book.

While there, Danielle Fleishman came to visit me and as soon as I showed her my vision of the book she became its biggest supporter. We went through countless revisions together, and she even drove down an inkjet printer from Portland so that I could proof pages while at the residency!

This book is a result of my casting a long a throw to Matt Love who helped me push the book to the next level with his enthusiasm and writer, guru, publisher knowledge. I won't ever forget initially showing him the book.

We met at Cafe Mundo in Nye Beach between lunch and dinner. I was so thrilled and nervous the whole drive down. I had been a fan of Matt's work for some time and now was about to meet him and hear what he had to say about the very elementary sketch of the forts book I was working on. In my frenzy trying to park and being a couple minutes late heading south from Lincoln City, I backed my car into a brand new black Prius. The woman from Otter Rock was just screaming at me and saying "Are you crazy?! What are you doing?!" I gave her my info and went inside. I was shook up but had to go inside, as I was already late. The waitress asked if I wanted a table and I said I was meeting someone. "Oh you're meeting Matt?! He's upstairs." Now I felt really nervous. I walked up. He was sitting by the balcony and got up and shook my hand, with a big grin

"James! How's it going? Want an iced tea?" And what followed was a friendship and collaboration, resulting in the expanded version of the book you are now holding.

And of course, without Don at Pacific Coast Books in Lincoln City, I probably never would've emailed Matt to begin with! Thank you for giving me his e-mail address and reassuring me that I had a good enough idea for a book to contact Matt and see what he thought.